#92-106

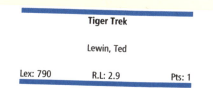

Tiger Trek

Lewin, Ted

Lex: 790   R.L: 2.9   Pts: 1

TIGER TREK

written and illustrated by TED LEWIN

Macmillan Publishing Company   New York
Collier Macmillan Publishers   London

For Trautie and Bodo Szonn,

and Fateh Singh Rathore.

Copyright © 1990 by Ted Lewin
Macmillan Publishing Company, 866 Third Avenue, New York, NY 10022
Collier Macmillan Canada, Inc.
Printed and bound in Japan   First American Edition

10   9   8   7   6   5   4   3   2   1

The text of this book is set in 14 point Trump Medieval.
The illustrations are rendered in watercolor on paper.
Library of Congress Cataloging-in-Publication Data
Lewin, Ted. Tiger trek/written and illustrated by Ted Lewin.
    p.   cm. Summary: Riding on the back of an elephant,
the author tours a wildlife park in India, observing the hunting
behavior of a mother tiger.
ISBN 0-02-757381-8
1. Tigers — Juvenile literature. [1. Wildlife refuges.
2. Tigers. 3. Animals.] I. Title.
QL737.C23L48 1990   599.74'428 — dc20
89-12710 CIP AC

A REAL-LIFE ADVENTURE IN INDIA

In India some of the hunting preserves of the old maharajahs have been turned into national parks. They still abound in tigers and other wild animals. The best way to see the animals is from the back of an elephant guided by its trainer, called a mahout.

Elephants and tigers respect each other in nature, so you are safe and secure in your box seat, called a howdah, fourteen feet above the ground.

The events in this real-life adventure story took place in Khana National Park in Central India and Ranthambore National Park in Rajasthan. Without these protected islands of habitat, these magnificent creatures would have no place left on earth.

Safe on the elephants' backs, we cross the river and amble into the early morning mists.

Dholes, the wild dogs of India, stop to wonder
at our elephants with their strange cargo.

High above in their leafy home,
a family of langur monkeys watches us.
A brand-new baby is especially curious.

A barasingha deer rakes up clumps of grass with
his horns. He wears the grass like a crown to impress
his mate and intimidate his rivals.

A short distance away, in the dark jungle,
a tiger sleeps.

She awakes and is hungry. She must hunt to feed herself and her cubs, hidden deep in the jungle.

As she begins to hunt, she melts into
the tall grass. She is almost invisible except
for the black and white of her ears.

She enters the ruins of an ancient palace
where a maharajah once lived.

From the crumbling wall of the palace,
she surveys the lake below.

Sambar deer feed on water weeds in the shallow lake, keeping a sharp eye for the tiger. They sense that she is hunting but feel secure in the water.

Passing by the wary sambar, the tiger reaches
the edge of the elephant grass.

A beautiful spotted deer, a chital, is feeding
near the elephant grass. It stamps its hoof
to alert the rest of the herd.

The tiger crouches and leaps.

A peacock screams an alarm.

The tiger takes her kill, a chital fawn, deep into the jungle.

In a few days she must hunt again. She may not be
so lucky the next time, but today she and her
family will eat. The chital's stamping has ceased,
and the peacocks are silent.